IT'S NOT *You*, IT'S *Me!*

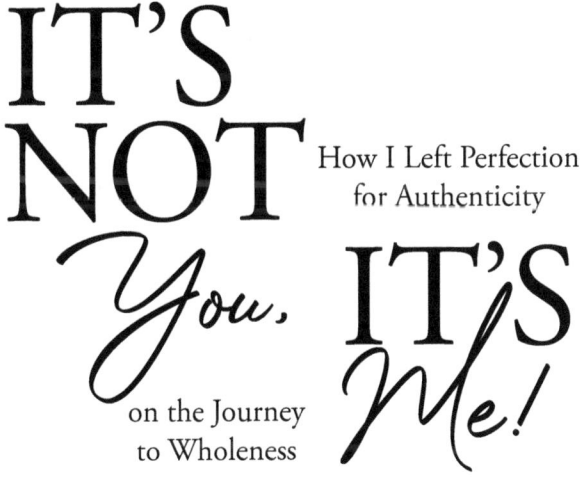

IT'S NOT *You,* IT'S *Me!*

How I Left Perfection for Authenticity on the Journey to Wholeness

DANARIUS HEMPHILL

IT'S NOT YOU; IT'S ME...

November Media Publishing, Chicago IL.
Copyright © 2022 Danarius Hemphill

All rights reserved. No part of this publication may be reproduced, distributed, or transmitted in any form or by any means, including photocopying, recording, or other electronic or mechanical methods, without the prior written permission of the publisher, except in the case of brief quotations embodied in critical reviews and certain other noncommercial uses permitted by copyright law. For permission requests, write to the publisher, addressed "Attention: Permissions Coordinator," at the email address below.

danarius_hemphill@yahoo.com

Ordering Information: Special discounts are available on quantity purchases by corporations, associations, and others. For details, contact the publisher at the email address above.

Printed in the United States of America

Produced & Published by November Media Publishing

ISBN: 979-8-9852149-5-6

TABLE OF CONTENTS

Preface 1

INTENTIONALITY

Don't Forget to Make your Bed 5
Isolation is Protection 7
Growth is your Right and Responsibility 9
Reboot Revamp Restart 12
Be Intentional Today 14
Consistency is a Bridge 16

SELF-REFLECTION

Success is Tied to Purpose 21
Past Mirror 23
Future Mirror 25
Embrace the Person in the Mirror 27
Terrified of Regret 30
Stop Making Permanent Decision Based on
Temporary Emotions 33
Transition Does Not Require Approval 35
Victim Mindset 37
"We blame all kinds of people for creating monsters.
Why not ourselves?" 39

KNOW YOUR WORTH

This Isn't What I Pictured 45
Living in Denial and Holding Yourself Hostage 47
Expiration Dates 49
Not Brand New Just Better 51
Don't You Dare Feel Unqualified – Take Back your
Confidence 54
Not Every Package is a Present 56

LOVE AND FRIENDSHIP

His Grace is Sufficient 61
Don't Let Loyalty Become Slavery 63
I'm Not Perfect, but I Serve a Perfect God 65
Don't Confuse Proximity with Relationships 67
Dare to Love 70

SEASONS

Troubled Waters 75
Old Keys Won't Open New Doors 76
I See It Now 78
The Breaking 80
The Deeper We Dig 82

SELF-CARE

The Pressure to Perform – Family 87
THE Pressure to Perform – Self 89

Recovering From Trauma 91
Saying No 93
Rest 94
Self-Care 96

CHANGING THE WORLD

Designated Survivor 101
Changed Thinking / Changed Life 103
The World Needs Game Changers 105
It Doesn't Have to Be Big. It Just Has to
Be Effective 107
Checkmate 109
Destiny Is Never Without Difficulty 111

AUTHENTICITY

Real Luxury in Inner Peace 115
Man Evolve 117
Wholeness/Go for Broke 119
Enough is Enough 121
The Lie and The Truth 123
Perfect vs. Authentic 125
Ask yourself if you have: Complete Control,
Some Control and or No Control 128
You Are a Masterpiece 130
Conclusion 132

PREFACE

The last few years of my life have been a journey, and it has taken me on an out-of-body experience. It has allowed me the precious opportunity to truly see myself. It took me a while to get there, but I am finally finding my voice after many years of feeling like I did not have one. I've learned, though, that my silence was not because I didn't have a voice; it was because I didn't know how to use it. Instead, I was using everyone else's voice instead of my own. I was speaking other people's thoughts and perceptions of me into existence instead of using my words to paint my self-portrait. See, it's a beautiful thing to connect to someone else's vision, but it's a truly fantastic thing to give birth to your voice and vision. It's an authentic version of you showing up in the world.

This thing that we call self-love has been an essential key to my success. It's me appreciating the stutter, the lazy eye, the learning impediments, all of me. In writing my first book, I had such a strong desire to get my story out that I failed to see how God was taking me on a journey of self-discovery. I had so many revelations in the process of writing that book. I discovered what happens when you keep secrets locked away inside of you. I discovered what happens when you stop being silent, even when everyone else doesn't approve. I learned what happens when you start knocking down walls and speaking your truth unapologetically.

But in this next chapter of life, this phase of genuine authenticity, I am happy to report that I have found my voice, and I will allow it to continuously bring forth authenticity in others and myself. I will use my voice to not only encourage, equip, and build up others, but also as the intersection between loving myself and helping others love themselves.

This book is my way of screaming, "WAKE UP!" Wake up your purpose. Wake up your destiny. It is time for you to recognize the full embodiment of who you are. There is no more waiting for permission or waiting for someone else to see you. There is an urgency, and all you need to meet that call on your life is God and your authentic self. It's time to wake up.

Intentionality

Freedom is useless if we don't exercise it as characters making choices... We are free to change the stories by which we live. Because we are genuine characters and not mere puppets, we can choose our defining stories. We can do so because we actively participate in creating our stories. We are co-authors as well as characters. Few things are as encouraging as the realization that things can be different and that we have a role in making them so.

—***Daniel Taylor***

Therefore, if we serve an intentional God, we should be intentional people. In what area of your life are you lacking intentionality?

DON'T FORGET TO MAKE YOUR BED

Growing up, my parents would always tell me to make my bed… and while it was the simplest thing I had to do all day, it was also the hardest. I just didn't see the point since I was going to mess it up again that night. As a grown man, I now see the value in making my bed in the morning. It sets the order for the day and how I will proceed. We spend 8 hours of the day at work, and many of us spend those 8 hours doing work that we don't enjoy. But even on the most challenging days, the one thing we have to look forward to is a clean made-up bed. It gives us a sense of accomplishment. We did what we were supposed to do, and now we can reap the benefits.

We tend to see success as this far-off unattainable goal that requires more than we can give, but it's the simple things we do that set us on a course for success. Unfortunately, we just don't want to do them. It makes me think of all the things I struggled to let go of – something I preferred to keep, even though letting go would be for my betterment. I had to start addressing the simple things in my life. Eventually, I realized that some of my most significant conflicts were within myself. We get so used to constantly hustling and grinding that we stop taking time to do the simple things in life. When we do those easy tasks initially, it shifts our mindset and puts us on a whole other paradigm to stay on track.

We are constantly moving from one battle to the next. That is the biggest trick of the enemy. It's not the battle. It's the feelings of wear and tears from fighting in battle. In the Bible, when David returned from battle, he found all the women and children were gone. They felt accomplished from their own battles but returned home to find their camp raided. He didn't even have a moment to bounce back and recover from battle before dealing with the next one. We have to position ourselves, so we aren't constantly preparing for the next battle. Even when trouble walks right up to your front door, sometimes you need to leave that door closed, stay inside, and deal with that problem when you are ready to deal with it. The enemy wants you worn out and on edge. He is betting that you won't ever fully recover. When we go from fight to fight to fight, we literally stay exhausted, and that allows the enemy to come in for the kill.

There has to be a time in our lives when we breathe and take a moment to bask in the season of what we have accomplished. We have to learn to say, "This is good, and I am going to enjoy it today. Tomorrow I will prepare for the battle ahead." We have to shift from the mindset of thinking there is always a fight or a battle to be won.

Enjoying our spoils may seem like a simple thing to do, but many of us never do it. I've earned three degrees, including a Ed.D, yet I have never taken the time to enjoy my accomplishments. Just like making your bed, taking the time to rejuvenate is a simple task that gives you the strength to handle the challenges of your day. Then, when the day is done, you can go home and melt into a nice clean bed.

ISOLATION IS PROTECTION

In 2020, many of us were unexpectedly thrown into isolation. For me, the initial thought of being isolated in my house felt like my demise. I'm a people person, so I saw it as a tactic of the enemy to destroy me. It wasn't until I was in the midst of isolation that I started seeing it differently. I moved from Detroit to Austin in the middle of the pandemic. I felt so alone at first. I felt like I didn't have anything or anybody to lean on in my new city. But over time, God used that quiet to establish me. Somewhere along the way, my isolation started to feel like a place of rejuvenation. I began to understand that God was using isolation to protect, preserve, and minister to me. He isolated me to hide me from the dangers that I could not see. I wanted to be out there doing this, that, and the other… but I didn't recognize the physical and emotional drain it was taking on my life. Old folks have a saying, "God had to sit me down to get me together." That's exactly what isolation is for me. It's God's way of sitting me down and making deposits into my spirit.

In isolation, God is able to show you and equip you for the journey ahead. I have learned so much during this time, and not all of it was easy to take. Have I found things I like about myself? Yeah. Have I found things that I need to work on about myself? Hell yeah. God has given me my best lessons in isolation. I could have still been in Detroit trying to please everyone and making myself more unhappy, but instead, I am enjoying the table that God has prepared for me. I watched the things that I thought might crush me ultimately become crushed.

Take a moment to step back and reevaluate the value of isolation. We sometimes miss the blessing when we're too close to it. Think about looking into your phone camera. When you are too close, you can't see your full self. You might only see your cheek or your eye. But when you step back, you can see the whole picture. As the entire world sat down for all those months, the earth started to rejuvenate. Oxygen levels increased, and polluted waters cleared – all because of isolation.

Stop being afraid of isolation. It is where you can find peace, solace, and rejuvenation. Open yourself to the blessings that can come from being alone. Too many people stay in toxic relationships out of the fear of being alone. They minimize their partner's toxic traits and rationalize the pain. There is a difference between being alone and being lonely. People embrace the noise of a toxic relationship because it keeps them from having to sit in isolation and deal with themselves – and it's not just relationships. We use all types of things to not deal with ourselves. For years, I used school to keep me from dealing with myself. As long as my mind was preoccupied with new information, assignments, and my dissertation, I did not have to look inside and fix my mess. But now that I have sat quietly, I know what is truly important and a priority in my life.

GROWTH IS YOUR RIGHT AND RESPONSIBILITY

Life is a journey that includes the ups, the downs, the good, the bad, the ugly, and the routine. I don't have to tell you about the ups and downs, but you may not be familiar with the routine. That is where we grow from the good, the bad, and the ugly. We tend not to associate growth with pain, anger, or hurt. But those experiences are often our greatest teachers. They launch us into the deep and allow us to experience the most significant amount of growth. When you're in the midst of routine, you can decide to be mad and stagnate there, or you can move forward by looking at it through a different set of lenses. We get so stuck in the good or the bad that we never move into the routine where the growth actually happens. It's the evolution that you never expected to come out of a good or bad situation. It is where you realize that the situation could have gone a whole other way. When we are in the midst of the highs and the lows, we can get so overwhelmed with what we are experiencing that we end up missing what God is trying to do in our lives. The routine is our opportunity for reflection and, ultimately, growth.

In the Bible, Joseph did not have to bless his brothers – the same ones who threw him into the pit, the same ones that rejected him, the same ones that weren't there for him, the same ones who lied to Joseph's father by telling him that Joseph was dead. Joseph had authority over them, and he didn't have to bless them, but he did. His actions showed two things… that God could trust Joseph and that, regardless of what he had been through and how much he may have wanted to get even, Joseph's mindset was still on blessing his brothers. He knew what his brothers meant for his evil; God meant for his good so that the nation could be blessed. Sometimes we get caught up in wanting God to punish a person for what they did to us, but your growth and your heart's posture have to be in the same place when you are seeking to have an impact.

Growth is not always solely about you. It is also entangled with the people whose lives are connected to your life. If we want to create a positive impact, we must understand that when we go through a difficult time, it may be about someone connected to our destiny. We have to be willing to use that growth and maturity to bless others. When God sees your growth and maturity, He can bless you with greater responsibility and power. Joseph had all of that power, and he could have refused to feed his brothers. But his posture was never from the standpoint of getting even. Instead, he said that, regardless of what they had done to him, he was still going to bless them. This is a great illustration of growth from a biblical standpoint.

Asking God to bless those who hurt you takes the weight off of you. Sometimes, you get so filled with anger that you stifle yourself from experiencing what's next. When carrying the weight of my hurt at my father and brother's hands, I felt like a ticking time bomb, but I had to grow out of that. When I started to change my perspective and began praying for God to bless them, I could feel God saying to me, "Now I can trust you with something. I can trust you with the next opportunity I'm about to bring your way. I can trust you with the next relationship I bring into your life. I can trust you because I know where you stand when it comes to serving people."

Whether people believe in God or don't believe in God, they are still His children. So, regardless of how people treat me, they are still the children of God. It is not my place to hate or despise them. I have one commandment only, which is to love my neighbor as I love myself. Sometimes it is easier said than done, but it is your responsibility, and when you start growing and changing your heart, you start to really see God show up.

REBOOT REVAMP RESTART

The people and situations that come into our lives can change us. They alter our hearts and even our minds, taking us so far away from ourselves that we lose sight of who we are truly called to be. As a result, we start making bad decisions and living our lives like we no longer know our worth. What do you do when your computer stops operating correctly and gets out of pocket? You reboot it, and that's what you need to do for yourself. When we feel far away from our true selves, we have to reboot to get back to our original design and function.

Once the reboot is complete, it's time to revamp. You must take the time to do the work and reevaluate what you are trying to achieve. Otherwise, you end up with the same unwanted outcomes that you have always gotten. You end up in the same toxic relationship over and over again because you choose the same person with a different face. You end up maxing out all of your credit cards because you choose Amazon over the therapy that you genuinely need. You get stuck in a job you hate because you are too afraid to further your education.

These harmful patterns can be broken when you stop making excuses and do the work to get things done. Now, I'm not saying that the work of revamping your life will be easy. It will definitely cost you some things. There will be moments when you desperately want to go back to what feels familiar and comfortable, but you have to remind yourself that what's ahead of you is so much better than what you left behind. What lies ahead of you is a healthy and happy relationship with someone who loves you just as much as you love them. The savings in the bank and a house to call your own lie ahead. What lies ahead is that new business you have always dreamed of owning.

That brings me to the final piece of this puzzle: Restart. Restarting is often seen as a bad thing, but it's not. Restarting means that you have learned the lessons and you are brave enough to try again. I've seen many business owners close the doors to their businesses. But what do they do? They reboot, revamp, and restart a whole new business that becomes a huge success. Who says that we can't do the same? That's why I don't believe in failing. I call it evolving. What we learn in one phase of our lives can show us what we need to know for the next phase of our lives.

Don't allow someone to tell you that it is not okay to stop and start again. Sometimes, you need that. If you want something different, you have to do some things differently, and that requires you to revamp, reboot, and restart.

BE INTENTIONAL TODAY

Intentionality is everything. We all need an agenda for what we want to accomplish and who we want to be. By starting each day with an intention about what you will or will not do in the hours ahead, you set things to avoid chaos and confusion.

Everything runs more smoothly with order. I remember when I held a fundraising event for a local men's shelter. I mapped out all of the necessary steps and followed through with each one. With that order and intentionality in place, the fundraiser was a success. It's the same with buying a house or applying for jobs; when things are in their proper place, they move more smoothly.

Intentionality brings order and requires you to be proactive about what you want to accomplish, who you are, and where you want to go. We all need a plan or a vision for who we want to be personally. Whether you use vision boards, words of affirmations, or positive sayings, you must be intentional with who you are from an authentic standpoint.

Now, setting your intentions will not keep all obstacles out of the road, but the intentionality of planning helps you consider some of those roadblocks in advance so you can allow room for them. A truly intentional person recognizes that the process is the process. They don't try to control every aspect of the process 100% of the time because they realize that they can't. Sometimes, those unexpected obstacles turn out to be the very breakthrough you were waiting for.

So, as you start your day, get your thoughts together and set your intentions. Take some time to consider where you want to go and what you want to achieve. Look at your authentic self and use that to set your intentions. Then, decide what you will do with your day to progress towards your goals.

CONSISTENCY IS A BRIDGE

I used to be so inconsistent in my life. I was a "fly by the seat of your pants" type of guy who never followed through with the things I said I wanted to do. But in the midst of my inconsistency, I learned the best lessons about being consistent. I couldn't blame anyone but myself for my actions (or inactions), and I eventually discovered that being inconsistent was not helping me grow and develop into my whole self. As I learned the importance of being consistent with myself and others, it allowed me to build more relationships. It gave me more room for the people and things that are a priority in my life.

It took me until my 30s to learn the importance of ensuring that my words and actions were consistent. The more consistent I was with myself, the more consistent I became in my relationships and meeting my goals. This is the bridge between wanting and achieving. Completing my doctorate required consistency. Buying my home needed consistency. Even this book is about the consistency of my brand. I have championed authenticity since starting my doctoral program, and it's a concept that remains very present in my message.

We cannot allow our inconsistencies to become a consistent part of our lives. When people see you as being inconsistent, they stop taking you seriously. They doubt your reliability and distrust your word. Do the work to ensure that you show up consistently in your life. Call yourself to the carpet and hold yourself accountable for your actions. By building your consistency, you also create a bridge to the life you dream of living.

Self-Reflection

You've still got time because you're still here. The goal was never perfection; it's completion. Let's take these unfinished stories that haunt us at night and put in the work required to discover the good promised to those who love God and are called according to His purpose.

—*Sarah Jakes Roberts*

The authentic version of you is closer than you realize, but it takes courage, might, fight, and will to be exceptional. Are you willing to look in the mirror and do the work?

SUCCESS IS TIED TO PURPOSE

Tell your secrets if you want to change the world and create an impact. Your success is tied to your purpose, and your purpose is often connected to your secrets, those painful experiences that you don't want anyone to know about. Your story of perseverance can be someone else's medicine, but you can't be a blessing if you keep your secrets from the world.

I love to pray. I love to worship. I love spending time with God, but I don't want everyone to know what goes on between God and me. We know God is omnipotent. We know that He is glorious, victorious, and triumphant, the alpha and omega. We know that he is amazing, but if we read the world, we see that God knows exactly what He's doing when he sends turmoil into our lives. I hate to say it like this, but God can be messy sometimes. He knew what He was doing when He told the man to marry the harlot, and every time she went back into the street, He told him to go back out there and get her. Messy. Things like that happened throughout the bible, but the biggest messes turned out to be the biggest blessings. It's as if God declared that no matter how messy I have to make it, I will get the glory.

Think about the art of creating pottery. When you make something, it is going to get messy. God is the potter, and we are the clay. We are not feeling the pain of it. The creator is feeling the pain. He is the one who has His hands in it. When things get hard, He has to smooth it out. When things are not rounding out to His will, He has to round it out a little more. In those moments, we may not know what He's doing, but He does.

We can even see this molding in the natural world. A mother can mold and shape a newborn baby's head. The head is the softest part of the baby, as it stretches during delivery and the mother can shape it. That's what God is doing with us. He is shaping us, which takes time, patience, and love.

For me, part of that shaping involved exposing what we have going on behind closed doors. It's as if God said to me, "We got a good thing going on, and I want people to know what you and I got going on." Without even realizing what was happening, I went from praying in the secret places of my life to opening up the services at church. Then, I went from worshipping in my secret places to leading the whole congregation in exaltation. Everything that God and I were doing in the confinement of my house began to carry out into my natural life. Even now, I serve my church and pastor as an armor bearer – and in every job I have had in the natural world, I have been an armor bearer for my supervisor. I am a servant, and who I am spiritually matches who I am naturally.

Your secret places are your gifts. They are your calling and your purpose. When all of those things are aligned, you will find your success.

PAST MIRROR

Most of us prefer to run from our past rather than face it. We want to forget about all of the hurt, anger, deception, and rejection that we experienced because it makes us uncomfortable and even ashamed. We are ashamed of the fact that – though some of our experiences could not have been prevented – plenty of them could have been if we had stayed focused instead of allowing outside things to come in and distract us.

But it's time to change our way of thinking when we look at our past mirror. Some of that hurt and pain pulled you back to launch you into your purpose. Being molested was an awful experience, but I would not know God the way I know God had I not been molested. That is my testimony.

If I hadn't been in toxic relationships, I would not know my worth. That is also my testimony. I remember someone asking me once, "So you think you're better than me?" Without missing a single beat, I replied, "Yes." Now, that wasn't from a place of arrogance. It was from a place of knowing my worth. I had to say goodbye to those toxic relationships to say hello to myself.

My past taught me how to appreciate myself and put me on a pedestal. I was trying to reach a mark that everyone had set for me, but I wasn't reaching for a mark that I set for myself. I wasn't creating my narrative because I kept doing the same things I had always done and expecting a different result. We all have so many mental issues and clouds in our heads that we never deal with. Ask yourself what kept you in that toxic relationship? What led you to be promiscuous? Why were you a yes man? What were you looking for?

If you never deal with these issues and address them, there comes a time when that chamber you thought was under lock, and the key becomes unlocked. It becomes a trigger for us, and we end up releasing something that we have never dealt with. The church always says to get our help from God, but some need to see a therapist. God got you covered, but you have to take the necessary steps to get the help you need. You don't want to carry your childhood trauma and the trauma of rejection and low esteem into your next. In this pandemic phase of your life, use those disinfection wipes you got stashed all over the house and start wiping some stuff down to get those germs out of your system.

FUTURE MIRROR

As you look at your future mirror, know that you have not even glimpsed the doors that will open in your life. A version of you will come forward and blow your mind but getting there requires that you show up and go off.

I have the privilege of working for the US Army Future Command. In performing our duties, we not only look at what has happened and what is currently happening, but we also look towards what's to come. We work to rapidly get our hands on the latest innovations and technologies, so we can make ourselves bigger, better, and faster. Every person needs to adopt the same strategy. Use the lessons of what you have been through and where you are now to suit up and equip yourself to become bigger, better, and faster in the days ahead.

God clearly states that our world is framed by the words that proceed from our mouths. We have the authority to declare something and believe it will be established. We can boldly say, "This is the outcome that I am looking for, and this is the outcome that I am going to get." When your life's plan aligns with God's plan for your life, nothing can keep it from coming to pass. Your world gets better, and your internal perspective improves because your happiness is no longer predicated on external things. It took a lot of work to change my inner perspective. I remember turning a whole wall in my home into a chalkboard. At the very top, I put a cup that symbolizes

God. I put the things that I wanted to accomplish at the bottom. I then placed strings from the cup down to each of those goals. This visualization reminded me that nothing I wanted to achieve would turn out right without that primary source. God needs to be at the center of it all, and when we place Him at the center, we begin to see things change in our favor.

We can change our outlook by adjusting our vision and preparing ourselves to accomplish it. I know it's cliché, but the future is bright, and we get to decide how things will end up. You must realize that you have more authority and power than you think. So often, we diminish our power because we have grown accustomed to not believing in ourselves, buying into the perspective that our voices don't matter.

Showing up and going off means recognizing your power and leaving it all on the table. It means giving the world everything that God has impregnated you with. Look at your future as being huge and grand. Look at the most seemingly impossible goals and say, "I can do that." It's about having a vision and making a plan. Without a vision, you don't know your future direction. Write it down. Say it. Declare it. Decree it. Announce it and shape it. As you look in your future mirror, recognize that it is time for you to show up and go off.

EMBRACE THE PERSON IN THE MIRROR

Take a look in the mirror. The person you see today represents every version of yourself from the different stages of your journey. It is a culmination of who you were, who you are, and who you will become, with each version bringing you understanding and insight into yourself. To reach a level of wholeness, you must accept and celebrate all three parts. Otherwise, you end up making the same mistakes over and over again. You'll never get to the best version of yourself because you keep flirting with the old versions.

Your current reflection can be a little tricky because it gives you a 20/20 hindsight view of who you were, along with just a glimpse of who you are destined to become. And if you focus on it too long, you can become too comfortable. You start thinking that, though you're nervous about what's to come, at least it isn't as bad as what used to be. You decide that it's okay to stay in the comfort of where you are instead of moving forward. Now, there's nothing wrong with being comfortable for a season, but seasons change. You can't just stay there once that change comes around. Even the best cut of meat starts to smell if you leave it out too long.

Life has a way of pushing you and giving you the nod that it is time for you to move. Don't let your comfort or fears keep you trapped in the present. Get the resources you need to move forward, including people who offer guidance and wisdom.

For years, I struggled with releasing the new version of me that was dying to get out. It was like the tug my dog puts me through on our walk every morning. He pulls the leash to go in the direction he wants, and I pull the leash back to keep him under my control. The version of who I was destined to be, was pulling me in one direction, while my fears about what would happen kept holding me back.

It wasn't about whether other people would like the evolved version of me. It was about whether I was going to like that version of myself. I pulled that chain that I kept on myself for so long that my hands became bloody. But I finally reached a stage in my life where I had to let it go. The time for pointing fingers at others was over. I finally accepted that my strength and deliverance depended on me. I had to look in the mirror and merge the past, present, and future versions of myself to elevate who I was destined to become.

After releasing all of it – flaws and all – I felt like everything I had been dreaming of and dying to change became possible. That's where wholeness comes in. Embracing the man in the mirror means breaking the patterns of destruction in my life, and it's an ongoing process. I am constantly reading books, talks, and sermons from other people who guide me on this journey.

Many of us walk around unprepared to release the person in the mirror, but we end up doing more damage than good by hesitating. The change you want to see in the world is tied to that version of yourself you won't release. Take this moment to accept what was and get excited about what's to come.

TERRIFIED OF REGRET

Nobody enjoys feeling regret. It can be painful to realize that you could have made a better choice. But there's a big difference between refusing to do something that you know you will regret and refusing to do things out of fear of regret. The regrets you know come from your past experiences and lessons learned. You don't avoid them out of fear; you avoid them out of wisdom and self-care. But the regrets you fear are the ones that could be holding you back from your true destiny.

Everything that we are destined to accomplish is already inside us. Most often, when we don't reach where we are trying to go, it's not because someone else was holding us back. It's because we were restricting ourselves from going the distance out of fear. When I realized that it was time to release what God put inside of me, it became clear that everything I needed had always been in me. I could accomplish everything I wanted to achieve as long as I kept going, even if I fell or got hurt in the process.

I do not want to ever look back on my life and say I wish I had. Even now, at the age of 35, I look at my life and wish I had traveled more, or I wish I had applied for that job. We have to stop letting our fears and insecurities hold us back. That glass ceiling that you have been trying to break. Those places you have been dying to go. If you step out on faith, you will not only see what you are capable of, but you will also tap into a version of yourself that you may not have known even existed. We have to move out of our way and go the distance anyway. In the same way that we talk ourselves out of things, we have to talk ourselves into making moves that could change our lives. We may even have to pressure ourselves to do what we ultimately want to do, from that job we want, that book we want to write, or that podcast we want to start.

That fear of regret you have is because you don't feel suited for your assignment. But what if the limits you place on yourself are what ultimately hold you back. Unlearn those limitations. You must get to a place where you encourage yourself to go the entire distance. Teach yourself a new way of thinking and reassure yourself that you can do and achieve things you never thought possible.

We often tell ourselves that it's too late. It's too far, or we're too old. We talked about all of those opportunities that passed us by. In reality, there are no missed opportunities. What's meant for you is meant for you. Even if you fail to seize the opportunity at the moment, it will ultimately present itself again. It may not look the same as the first time, but it will come back because opportunities are attached to our destiny. When you start to believe this in your heart, you realize that regret is a waste of time. It mentally drains you. If we go ahead and do it, even if it doesn't go as planned, we can still say that we did our best.

A few years ago, I ran for a seat on the local school board. I campaigned solely based on social media and got a few thousand votes, but I did not win. Here is the kicker, though. I only ran for the school board because I was too afraid to run for the state senate, which I wanted to do. I feared losing and regretting my decision to run. But if I had gone for what I was called to do, I probably would have won that state senate race. Instead, I put limitations and restrictions on myself. I was so afraid of succeeding in that space that I talked myself out of going after what I really wanted. Now, I regretted that for a long time, but I had to let that regret go ultimately. It wasn't a missed opportunity. It was a setup for my next campaign. I know the opportunity will eventually come around for me again, and I will take it.

We all have regrets, but it is time to address them. Do it anyway. Try it anyway. So, what if you don't get it right? So, what if you aren't perfect? We have all been in positions where we question whether we are good enough, but you'll never know if you don't go after it.

STOP MAKING PERMANENT DECISION BASED ON TEMPORARY EMOTIONS

Your emotions will have you acting a fool out here in these streets, period. Listening to your feelings will have you in the wrong relationship, in the wrong place, and at the wrong time. Emotions will have you doing things that you really should not be doing. Let me tell you this right now. Don't trust them! You have to put your emotions in check before they check you.

I don't rely on my emotions. To be honest, they can have me acting childish and petty sometimes. If I get wrapped up in my feelings, they will leave me out here, focusing on the wrong things. So many times, I allowed my emotions to dictate my life. Then, when I looked back on the terrible choices I made, it left me feeling broken down, confused, and disappointed in myself for relying on temporary feelings to make life-changing decisions.

You have to learn how to deal with your emotions if you want long-term stability. We allow our feelings to imprison us and make us slaves to unhealthy things. Your emotions will have you without a job… all because of how you perceived or interpreted a situation with a coworker. Your emotions will have you laying hands on somebody and all of the consequences that come along with that. People make terrible decisions based on how they feel at any given moment. They will go around sleeping with Tom, Dick, and Harry because their emotions tell them they need to feel wanted. Emotions will have you buy a Louis purse instead of paying your water bill or buying a car you can't afford.

I hear people saying, "Live your best life!" and there's nothing wrong with that. But living your best life doesn't mean allowing your emotions to take over your good sense. You have to keep control of your feelings before they take control of your life.

TRANSITION DOES NOT REQUIRE APPROVAL

When God is ready to take you to that next level, He will not wait for your approval. He does not need, nor require, you to say yes because transition happens whether you are ready or not. Think about those times in your life when you tried to pull away from God… those times when you thought your will was stronger than His will. Didn't you ultimately end up doing His will anyway? That was the yes that you didn't even realize you said.

I can't tell you how often I told God I didn't want to do something because I didn't think I was smart enough or eloquent enough. But I always ended up doing it anyway. You can't let fear or insecurity stop you from following God's plan for your life. When you tap into those fears, you'll probably discover that you are far more capable than you thought. Ultimately, when God sets a course for our lives, He will make sure that we stay on track for that thing to happen. Think about Moses and all of the stages in life he had to go through to deliver God's message. He went from being into a river to living in a king's palace. Then, he had to leave the familiarity of his home and move towards the unfamiliar to reach his destiny. In moments of uncertainty, we discover who we are meant to be from a destiny standpoint.

The whole world is experiencing a transitional season right now with the pandemic, police violence, and all of these senseless deaths. The Supreme Court of Heaven says, "Let my people go." When you constantly oppress a group of people, those people will rise and take back what that nation has taken from them. We are seeing a generation saying no more. They declare that it is time to stop these premature abortions of their ultimate destiny. This transition is happening without the government's approval or the powers that be. It's happening because God is ordaining it, and no one will be able to stop it.

Transition doesn't take something out of you that is not already there. So many of us fail to see how special we are, even when everyone around us can see it. We look closely in the mirror, and all we see are imperfections. So, when a transitional season arrives, we disapprove because we feel ill-equipped to handle the change. But God sees the fullness of who we are, and He allows the people around you to see it too. Through life's transitions, we begin to appreciate the fullness of who we are truly. We start to see the big picture. So, the next time God brings a season of transition into your life, don't resist it. Know that it will happen with or without your approval, so embrace the change and trust in His plan.

VICTIM MINDSET

We wake up every day with the ability to make choices about our lives. We can choose to do what's right for us, or we can choose to do things that ultimately hurt us. We can live in our power or stay in a mindset that keeps us down. Being molested, rejected, and counted out made me think less of myself. I stopped anticipating good things coming into my life and instead started expecting the short end of the stick. This is where we end up when we let our experiences define the world we live in… when we let those experiences tell us that we will never do or be more than what we have always been. I bought into a belief that I was a victim who could never grow outside of my negative experiences. I had to start telling myself a new story. I had to tell myself that I was smart, brilliant, handsome, and capable. I had to start believing in myself.

We all have to reach a place where we are no longer enslaved to ideas, thoughts, and theories about ourselves. Our experiences are just that. Experiences. They don't determine who we are as individuals. We experience things, and we learn from them. Life is filled with journeys and challenges that we all must go through. But in those moments, we can choose whether we will be a victim or a victor.

The Bible says that people are overcome with the words of their testimony. Your experiences become your testimony, but how are you using them? Are you allowing them to keep you down, or are you using them to build yourself and others up? When I thought I was being knocked out or pulled back, God was getting ready to push me forward. Sometimes a knockout is not a knockout. It's a comeback. Once I realized this concept, I began to utilize the experiences that could have taken me down as launching pads to propel me further and encourage someone else. When bad things would happen in my life, I began asking myself a question. Are you going to sit here and keep crying over spilled milk, or are you going to move? My mom always taught me that it was okay to cry for a moment. Then, it was time to brush the dirt off and keep going. Put those victim mindsets away and use your experiences to push you farther.

Remember that the fight is fixed for you to win regardless. You were chosen by God for this life. You were chosen to navigate through all of your experiences. Nothing that you are going through will break you… not those drugs, that alcohol, or those bad habits. You can come back from that if you shed that victim mindset and allow yourself to be launched into your purpose.

"WE BLAME ALL KINDS OF PEOPLE FOR CREATING MONSTERS. WHY NOT OURSELVES?"

I used to binge-watch the television show "Law & Order: SVU." As a survivor of sexual abuse, I have always been interested in the stories they bring to the screen. In one episode, the characters Benson and Stabler were talking about possible suspects when Stabler said, "We blame all kinds of people for creating monsters. Why not ourselves?" That question got me thinking about my own life.

It's easy to point fingers at people who did this, that, or the other to us. But we never have conversations about the person inside who holds us back. We never deal with the enemy inside of us that is us. They examine the crime scene on those crime shows, check fingerprints, and go through forensics science to find the criminal. I had to learn how to step back and examine the person who ultimately hindered me from reaching my goals. I had to examine why I didn't feel confident about operating in the areas where I am gifted and skilled. I had to examine why I am always extra critical of myself and why I use a fine-tooth comb when it comes to what I think I can and cannot do.

We have to stop flirting with what we are trying to kill and kill it. This is a big issue for a lot of us. We are called to address the things that stress us out, but instead of dealing with them, we choose to flirt with them. We put our toes in it like a pool of water and declare, "I can deal with it this much." Then, when it gets out of control, we want to step back and remove ourselves from it altogether. My dad would say that lust starts small, but the more you feed it, the bigger it gets, and the bigger it gets, the more out of control it becomes.

As I matured, I realized that things were not working out the way I planned because I was looking for something I could no longer put my toe in and deal with a little bit. Toxic traits like procrastination, overanalyzing, feelings of being unworthy and not smart enough. Those aren't the voices of others saying I'm not good enough. It is literally looking at me and telling myself what I can't do with my life. But those voices must be silenced.

We are all made up of stories, and each day we experience a whole new one. The only way we can get to the place we need to be is by redefining the narrative about ourselves. You have to tell yourself a whole other story. That was my issue. In fact, I am still learning how to change the narrative. I'm learning how to encourage myself and change the whole story. It's an ongoing struggle but necessary for survival. That old story leads to depression and suicidal thoughts. It keeps you from reaching your purpose because you always have that "woe is me" narrative running through your head.

Look at yourself under another microscope. Look past all of the lies you tell yourself and examine the person you are meant to be in this world. I know life can look messy sometimes, but that mess is just the enemy inside you. You can find yourself. You're not too messy, and you're never too messed up.

I recognize the demons I created. I am learning how to dethrone insecurities. I am learning how to dethrone low self-esteem. I am learning how to dethrone people taking advantage of me and being mistreated. I am learning how to appreciate myself. At 35 years old, I am just getting to a place where I can say; this is me. And I am going to appreciate him.

Know Your Worth

You deserve better… but you'll have to go
get it. No one can bring it to you.

—*Sherrayna Coleman*

On the road to discovering our self-worth,
we cannot afford any distractions. What distractions
are keeping you from recognizing your worth?

THIS ISN'T WHAT
I PICTURED

In December of 2016, I stood in an auditorium waiting to cross the stage for the hooding ceremony of my doctoral degree. It was the finale of a long educational journey. Years of blood, sweat, and tears had gone into this moment. I was just a Black boy from Detroit who grew up with a speech impediment. I was someone who doctors labeled mentally retarded at the age of five. I was someone who read below my grade level for years. I was someone who had been molested and abused. Everything was stacked against me.

Yet, there I stood. A Black man from Detroit who had earned five degrees, broken generational curses, and built a bridge for my family to move from the present into the future. All before reaching 30 years old. But as I stood in the midst of one of the most accomplished and celebratory moments of my life, I felt overwhelmingly anxious and undeserving.

I thought that earning that degree would catapult me into my destiny. I thought I would finally be worthy in the eyes of the world. But as I stood there with tears running down my face, a wave of uncomfortable truth washed over me. There would be no more books, lectures, and dissertations to distract me from reality. I was now fair game to all of the issues in my life, and it was terrifying.

I was displeased and dissatisfied with myself. I had been so wrapped up with the external things that I had no time to work on my internal issues. So, now what? Where was I going to go from here? School had offered me a safe haven, but in the end, it wasn't the thing that was going to change my family's legacy. It wasn't the degrees. It wasn't the title or finally becoming a doctor.

Instead, it was the beginning of a new season. It was time to put away the schoolwork and get to work on me. I had to deal with myself and face the past hurts. I realized that who I thought I was and wanted to be was not who God was calling me to be. It was time to establish Danarius in this season.

It wasn't what I pictured because I thought my life would be set on a specific trajectory. I was hoping that the successes of my education would make things easier, but in actuality, it was lonely at the top, and I'm not even at the top.

LIVING IN DENIAL AND HOLDING YOURSELF HOSTAGE

There was a time in my life when the person that I thought I was didn't line up with the person I was. I thought I wasn't hurt. I thought I wasn't angry. I thought I wasn't bitter. But I realized that all of that played a role in my life. I kept telling myself that I couldn't be that mad, but that anger eventually got to a point where I couldn't manage it any longer.

When I look back at my past mirror, I realize how uncomfortable I was in my own skin. I hated my speech impediment, my voice, and my big teeth. I was not comfortable with anything about myself. I didn't think I was handsome enough, intelligent enough, or articulate enough. I was uncomfortable with the Danarius that God created, and those feelings hindered me from recognizing my true purpose and future. I saw my shortcomings as disqualifications. Yet, as I looked around at other people, I saw them as intelligent, capable, and equipped for greatness.

Instead of embracing my reality, I held myself hostage to my self-denial and allowed other people to define me. I finally started recognizing my impediments as my gifts. My long list of shortcomings are the things that make me beautiful and unique. God can only bless who he created you to be, not who you pretend to be. I wasted so much time acting like I had it all together that I lost myself. God was saying, "I don't see Me. I see someone completely different, and until who I created shows up, I can't give you what I want to give you."

I realized that I should have accepted all parts of myself all of the time, from my big teeth and speech impediment, to my feelings of hurt and anger. I had to stop living in denial before I could stop holding myself hostage.

EXPIRATION DATES

To get to who we are destined to be, we have to get through who we are not destined to be, and that can mean wrestling through confusion on the journey to finding clarity. So many of us carry around these ideas of who we think we are. We carry them around for so long that we start to buy into them. We spend our time and energy trying to reach this unattainable goal instead of working to reach a direct connection with who we are destined to be. We have to give that illusion of who we think we are an expiration date.

God can't bless who you pretend to be. He can only bless who He has called you to be. And the more you attempt to travel down a road of illusions, the farther away your destiny lies. God is ready to bless you right now, but you refuse to tap into whom He has blessed you to be. What are you waiting for? Are you guilty of comparing yourself to others, thinking that you need their skill sets to be great? I confess that I have done this in my life. Even now, others tell me that they see who I am destined to be, but I have trouble seeing it for myself. I keep buying into this illusion that I don't possess the skills to be who I am destined to be. But I have to give an expiration date to who I think I am to tap into who I am really called to be.

You have to realize that you are great at what God has called you to do, just as others are great at what God has called them unto. Stop judging yourself based on other people's reflections and start seeing yourself through God's direction and illustration. A breaking happens when you know it is time for those illusions to expire. Tiredness and exhaustion push you to move towards your destiny. The emptiness that comes from crafting yourself based on everyone else turns into a voracious hunger to discover who you truly are. It doesn't matter what you feed it. It doesn't matter what vices you give it or how high you get. There must be a separation between what is real and what is not, what I am called to be and what I am not called to be, who I am destined to be and who I am not destined to be. Until you give that falsehood an expiration date, you will never be able to tap into your destiny. There will be this endless nagging of something that eludes you. Give it an expiration date. Stop prolonging, hindering, and stagnating what God wants to do in your life.

NOT BRAND NEW JUST BETTER

When people tell me, "You're acting brand new," my response is always, "No. I'm not new. I'm just better." It took me a while to get to that place, but I realized that their opinion of me and what I'm doing in my life is more about their issues than mine. When people accuse you of acting "brand new," they are accusing you of thinking you are somehow better than them. But I don't think I'm better than anybody. It's not a competition. The only person I compete with is myself, so when I say I'm better, what I mean is that my experiences and God's grace have made me better than the person I used to be.

I can't lie. It was hurtful the first time I heard someone say that about me, especially since some of my closest friends were there. It made me question myself. Yes, I was moving differently and in a different space, but I thought that was a good thing. The words of a very wise person put it into perspective for me. He told me that they had grown accustomed to me being at a lower level, and when I began to elevate, that was a problem for them. See, it was okay for them to elevate to a new level, but I was supposed to stay in my place because that made them feel comfortable. They wanted me at that level because they could walk over me. They could talk to me disrespectfully. They could mistreat me, and they knew I would not respond.

But as I began to grow, I recognized my value and realized that real friends are not supposed to treat each other that way.

There was no reciprocity. I constantly supported and celebrated them, but they would never show up for me. They resented my growth. I had done more with so much less than what they had been given in life. I was a young man from Detroit's west side whose father was on drugs and mother could barely make ends meet. Yet, even with far fewer resources than they had, I could make it to the same financial level that they were on. Again, they were comfortable with me at the lower level but not at a higher level. It was hurtful, but it gave me the power to cut that negativity out of my life. Those so-called friends are no longer a factor in my life. I finally saw them at face value.

Some people don't want you to reach certain plateaus because they don't want to feel like they live in your shadow. I have had friends who I thought would always be there for my journey, but when I started accomplishing things, they made it clear that they were not prepared to go with me to the next level. Instead, they tried to hold me back and refused to celebrate my wins. If you care for me as much as I care for you, you have to be involved in my journey, the good and the bad, and root for my success. I realized that my vision and dream for my life wasn't their dream for me.

I wasn't acting brand new. My experiences just made me better, and they didn't like that. The way that those people treated me, did me, walked over me, and mistreated me made me better. So, the next time somebody tells you that you're acting brand new, thank them for pushing you to your new level where you can be better than you have ever been before.

DON'T YOU DARE FEEL UNQUALIFIED – TAKE BACK YOUR CONFIDENCE

So many people walk around feeling like they are unqualified for life. We doubt our abilities. We doubt our talents, allowing outside people to shape how we see ourselves. Then, when we don't reach our goals, we point the finger and blame this person or that person instead of taking responsibility for ourselves.

Before you can reclaim your confidence, you must look inside yourself. Examine what is about you, or the things connected to you, that hold you back from reaching your purpose. What keeps you from moving towards everything you want to accomplish. Whatever you want your life to be, you have to give birth to that, and as any mother will tell you, giving birth is not a painless process.

There is no door that any man can shut to keep you from getting where you want to go. When I wanted to go to Wayne State to get my Ph.D., they said no. They told me that I would have to go back to undergrad to get another education degree. If I had stopped at that shut door, I would have never gone on to accomplish my goal of earning two degrees and becoming the first Ed.D. in my family. If I had believed what Wayne State said to me, I would have stopped there and missed out on all the rewards that came from my perseverance.

How did I find the strength to keep going? I got to a place where I realized that a no on earth does not equate to a no in God's eyes. You have to decipher between man's no and God's no. If God is telling you no, it's a done deal. But when a man tells you no after God has said yes, you have to pursue that thing with all diligence. Life had said no to me so many times that I figured it was past time for life to offer me up a yes. When Wayne State told me what I could not accomplish, it reminded me of the many times that I had been told I wasn't good enough. I told God that if He allowed me this opportunity, I would bless His name by showing others the potential they don't see in themselves. I would exemplify that people's lives are not decided by standardized testing. I would show people that they can go from the hood to the hills and accomplish all the things society tells them they cannot achieve.

When I decided that I wanted what God wanted for me, I gained confidence in the world and let those feelings of inadequacy go. When your will aligns with God's will, there is no devil in hell that can get in the way. Let those closed doors become your motivation. Use that no to push you to the next place and open the next door. It is that yes in your spirit and that gut feeling that tells you where you are supposed to be in your life, so don't you dare feel unqualified. Take back your confidence, and don't let anything keep you from your dreams.

NOT EVERY PACKAGE IS A PRESENT

I have become very fond of shopping online. I get excited when that doorbell rings, and I know there's a package waiting for me on the other side of the door. Sometimes, I excitedly open the package only to find that it is not what I ordered. I can't tell you how many shorts and workout clothes I've bought that ended up being so small that they stopped my blood circulation. I quickly learned that every package is not a present.

Every friendship, job, whatever new thing comes into your life… may not ultimately be what you expect it to be. You may have to reassess and ask yourself whether it is what you want and need. Ask yourself if this is where you really want to invest your time.

Maybe you choose something that will please you for the moment but won't sustain you for the long term. For instance, getting a job is the easy part. But once they get you in, you have to demonstrate what you know in an environment that may not support your needs. Things aren't always what we expect them to be, and sometimes what we need doesn't come in the type of package we expect. That good man may not come with a six-pack and a smile. That worthy woman may not have a Coca-Cola bottle figure. But each of those packages can still be an amazing present. You can't go into a relationship withholding honor and respect because that person isn't shaped into the form you expected. On the flip side, what we think will be a present may be the devil. The person who looks so good on the outside could end up being your worst nightmare.

It's all about our expectations. When we learn to value what is truly important and stop judging based on outward appearance, we can better discern which packages are presents and which ones are best left alone.

Love and Friendship

You are loved today, tomorrow, and always!

—Unknown

Are they worthy of your love?

HIS GRACE IS SUFFICIENT

Life has taught me countless times that God's grace is sufficient. There have been so many things that I got myself into and didn't know how to get myself out of, but God always gave me the grace I needed to get through. Toxic work environments, toxic relationships, turmoil in my home, one-sided friendships. Looking back, I know that I could not have overcome any of those things without God's merciful grace. Even in the darkest places of my past, when I thought that death was a better option than anything God had in store for me in the future, He wrapped me in His grace. He reassured me that my current circumstances were no indication of where He was about to take me. He showed me that even though it was a season of difficulty, it was not a season for quitting.

When you have gone through hell and back, been rejected by your friends, and ostracized from your family, that is when God's grace shows up. For me, it showed up when I finally decided to leave a toxic relationship, and God promoted me to a new opportunity in a new city. It showed up when, despite my learning disability, God matriculated me through the halls of higher education. His grace showed up when He gave me a village to fill the space created by the loss of my biological father. Even at my deepest levels of pain, God was always there to bless me with His grace.

God's grace for you is designated just for you. At every level and stage of your life, He applies the measure of grace that you need to get through. When God applies His grace to you, there is no restriction to that which you can overcome.

DON'T LET LOYALTY BECOME SLAVERY

I am a servant of people at my core, but sometimes I get so wrapped up in helping other people that I lose who I am. I have found myself serving people and being taken advantage of by them. It began to feel like slavery because they only wanted me present when it benefitted them. In their eyes, I was only worth what they needed from me. I think about all of the friendships I wanted to grow and mature, but many of those people only called on me when they needed something, even if it had been years since we last talked. They only wanted to interact with me when I was the best option for meeting their immediate needs. There were no messages to say hello or calls to check on me. I wasn't getting any of that from the majority of my relationships.

Out of loyalty, I spent my time and energy trying to save somebody when that wasn't what God had called me to do. I kept ending up in relationships that God had not designated me to be in with people who did not value my friendship. They were distractions from my destiny. I could not see the people who were meant for me because I was too focused on people who were taking advantage of me.

My mom has often said to me, "If they don't deserve, they just don't deserve you." She told me that I should not give my loyalty to people who did not deserve it. I had to learn how to accept people for who and where they are in their lives. The more I began to change, grow, and evolve, the more I came to a level of appreciation for the people who loved me authentically. You have to be picky with who receives your loyalty. You have to manage your relationships and not allow your relationships to manage you.

When you find yourself in these relationships, recognize that these unhealthy relationships only exist because you allow them. Only you can keep yourself from becoming enslaved to relationships in which you don't have any business. Think about what you hope to gain from these relationships. Is it appreciation? Maybe it's someone to honor you as much as you honor them. Some people don't even know how to do that, so why are you allowing your loyalty to become slavery?

I'M NOT PERFECT, BUT I SERVE A PERFECT GOD

The beauty of not being perfect is, "Who said we gotta be perfect?" We were never called to be perfect. There is no perfect human, which is why the enemy despises us. While the angels were created to be perfect, the man was not. Satan was jealous of God's undying love for such imperfect people. The requirement was never to be perfect. The requirement was always to be authentic. God can't bless who we pretend to be. He can only bless who He created us to be. He wants to see himself in all of us. When we give up this need for perfection, we can reach who we are authentically destined to become.

Even in the church, I love a new person because they go all the way in. They aren't trying to appear perfect to everyone around them and half-stepping their commitment to God. The Christians who have been saved for 20 plus years make you question whether or not they are truly saved. Those babes in Christ are not trying to be perfect. They are just trying to get it together.

I have learned, and I'm still learning, that I don't have to be perfect. I don't have to be perfect at my job. I don't have to be perfect in my family. I don't even have to be perfect in my church because the church is made up of imperfect people, and that's why it's the church. There are imperfect people throughout the bible… David, Mary, Joseph, and John. I look at all of them, and I recognize that none of them reached the plateau of perfection. It's all about evolving, and we don't have to be perfect because we serve a perfect God who doesn't sleep and doesn't slumber. He is always here with us at his forethought. When thinking of being perfect, you are trying to equate yourself to God. He doesn't need you to be perfect. He just needs you to show up with all of your flaws and be your authentic self.

DON'T CONFUSE PROXIMITY WITH RELATIONSHIPS

We often make the mistake of confusing proximity with relationships. We form lasting connections with people who come into our lives without realizing the negative effect. Then, once we fall into these relationships, we allow these people to mistreat us over and over again, only to repeatedly forgive them out of desperation to maintain the relationship. We allow an ongoing cycle of disrespect because we confuse proximity with a relationship.

After years of enduring these toxic situations, I learned to vet people as they came into my life. I assess them before connecting instead of waiting until later to learn the truth. First, I need to determine their motive. I need to know their agenda and why they want to be connected with me. I analyze the situation to determine if I want and need to be connected to this person. If not, I disconnect myself earlier rather than later.

I've also learned to put people in their proper places. Not everyone is a true confidant. Most of the people in your proximity are undeserving of your authenticity and transparency. Some people only deserve the surface, and you leave it right there to protect your peace. When people are constantly taking withdrawals out of your life without making deposits, you end up becoming overdrawn, just like a checking account.

You also have to identify your Judas. Jesus had 12 disciples, and even though one was the devil, He considered all of them his friends. Judas was able to do something that the other disciples could not. He was able to push Jesus into his divinity. Some people are there to push you towards your purpose in life. If you find your Judas, you will find your destiny. Subliminally tell that person, "I need you to betray me and do what you are going to do, so that you can push me into my divinity." The most painful and traumatic relationship of my life resulted in my being molested, but I would never be who I am now if I hadn't experienced it. Judas relationships can push you to honor and respect yourself more.

Your Judas probably doesn't even know they are teaching you a lesson. They are just along for a ride. You may even be somebody's Judas. You may think you are doing your best by someone, but you're doing something totally different from their perspective. God orchestrates all of this, and He may put us into somebody's life to do what we think is correct, but it's pushing them into their necessary season.

Just because someone is in your circle doesn't mean they have your best interest in mind. You can't be authentic with everyone in your proximity. Sometimes people don't know why they want to be connected to you. They may be attracted to your anointing, your energy, and your vibe. But just because they are attracted to you, it doesn't mean that you are destined to be connected forever, or even at all.

Your peace and energy are precious. Stop sharing them with everyone in your proximity. Save your relationships for the people who truly deserve them.

DARE TO LOVE

Our current society has made sex too easy and relationships too difficult. Far too many people have no intention of paying the price for true love. They don't want to look past the physical aspects, and they aren't willing to sacrifice their wants and needs for the other person. My mother always told me that her greatest competition was trying to "out love" my dad. She called it a competition that partners should want to have. If you come in here with a dozen roses, I am coming in here with three dozen roses next week. I see your try, and I raise it. It says to your partner that you understand the assignment of loving them, and you are willing to take it on.

I am guilty of shutting the door and deciding that love doesn't live here anymore. But late in the midnight hour, I hear my heart longing for someone to cuddle with, grow with, and share my life with. And I want that. I always have, but I was afraid of it. So, I wasn't allowing myself to be loved. I had to learn what love was not before preparing myself to love again. I had to get past the idea of what people said love was to realize what true authentic love is.

My previous relationships made me feel like I didn't deserve to be loved and genuinely cared for. I had to learn to love myself and to recognize true love. It's a lesson I learn daily by looking at how God wakes me up and protects me, and stays with me when I'm alone. I learn it by seeing how my mom and family look at me with happiness and pride. I even learn it from how my dog looks with those loving eyes. As I learn these things, it gives me the courage to try love again.

I am removing all of that anger, hurt, and disappointment so I can be ready to try again when the right one comes along. There won't be any more "just anyone." It must be the right one. I know it won't be easy, but I also know that I have to overcome my fear and dare to love.

When God is taking you through a shift, you have to be prepared to be misidentified.

—Pastor Donald Coleman Sr.

———————————————

Seasons prepare us for what is coming next. Are you ready?

TROUBLED WATERS

I am specifically speaking to my fellow millennials with this word, but I believe there are important lessons for everyone regardless of age. We, as a generation, need to trouble the water. We need to upset the balance and the environment of what is going on around us. When you think about these movements currently taking place, they are being pushed by people who are unapologetically troubling the waters. They challenge the social norms of what we have become accustomed to within our society. Many people disagree with their methods, but they don't let that cloud their vision. They know that they must trouble the water to reassess the current establishment and bring about necessary changes.

Our society, and our world, need individuals who are willing to trouble the water. Look at Rahab in the bible. She was a prostitute who became a biblical hero because she was willing to trouble the water and help the spies take Jericho. Look at the civil rights icon Rosa Parks. She decided that enough was enough, and she took action. As I look at where we are today, I don't see enough of us declaring that enough is enough. There aren't enough of us to serve and solve with a burning feeling inside. The thing that bothers you the most is probably the thing that you have been called in to trouble. Take that passion and use it to trouble the water.

OLD KEYS WON'T OPEN NEW DOORS

I've had many cars in my lifetime, including two BMWs and three Jeeps. Whenever I bought a new car, even when it was the same make and model, the old keys would not open the new car doors. I could hit unlock or try the AutoStart button. It would not work. When I purchased my house, I sometimes would mistakenly try to use the keys for my mother's house to unlock my door... and they never once worked. Those keys were set and designated to work at the level where I received them. When I progressed to a new level, I needed new keys because old keys won't open new doors. It just doesn't work.

When God presented me with new levels and new opportunities, I had to leave behind my way of thinking to move forward. We tend to hold on to things longer than we ought to. It could be clothes we can no longer wear or paperwork we no longer need. We hold on to things that we should have let go of a long time ago, and it keeps us from moving forward. Familiarity can make you stagnant sometimes. Think about eagles. When it's time for their eaglets to get out of the nest, the mother makes it uncomfortable for them to be there, and if she has to, she will push them out to either fall or soar. If they look like they aren't going to make it, she will go down there and save them, but first, they must at least try to soar.

When God elevates you, you have to take the leap and be prepared to soar on a level you have never soared before. You have to leave that old way of thinking behind. New doors require new keys, so you have to elevate your thoughts and faith. God wants a whole new praise from you at this level. He wants you to dig deeper and move away from what feels familiar. What worked on one level may not be sufficient for the next level.

So, when it comes time to open new doors, you have to shift your frame of thinking and your level of expectation. You have to expect and believe that when you turn the doorknob to your new home, or start this new relationship, or accept this work promotion, that the season is going to be different. We ask God for things, and when He gives them to us, we act like we aren't ready for them. Get ready. Prepare yourself to trade in those old keys for brand new ones.

I SEE IT NOW

Remember that time when you didn't get that job… when you didn't get that promotion… when that relationship broke your heart… when you didn't get the loan to buy that house. Sometimes we have a desire for something, but we only have a glimpse of what we think it is. We don't have a complete picture of what it truly is or how it will impact our peace of mind. We know we want it. We think we need it and we have to have it now.

Reflecting on my life since writing my previous book, I realize that I have learned a lot about myself. I can see the differences in my life when I stopped being extra hard and overcritical of myself. I've had the opportunity to go places and do things I never thought I would have the chance to do. I see now that the only thing ever holding me back was my inability to move my fears out of the way. Fear plagued my life for so long. Instead of aggressively pursuing the desires of my heart, I wasted time questioning whether every single move would be the correct one. I now know that making the wrong move doesn't hinder you. Instead, it adds to your toolbox and your ability to kick fear out of the way. I lived in a constant state of could have, would have, should have. But I now see what it means to embrace the fear and do it anyway.

Don't be restricted to your small way of thinking or hold yourself hostage, to the "what ifs" of not getting everything right. Nobody is an overnight success. The most accomplished person in the world made mistakes along the road to achieving their dreams. You cheat yourself out of your purpose when you allow fear, opposition, and discontentment to take hold. Stop cheating on yourself.

As I matured, I began to see that just because things don't go the way I want or don't happen in my time, that doesn't mean that they are not promised or due unto me. Love yourself, trust yourself, and see the value of moving ahead in the face of fear.

THE BREAKING

There have been a lot of times in my life when I have felt broken and completely shattered. Some of those times were caused by something that someone did to me. Other times were because of something I did to myself. Sometimes the breaking was physical. Other times, it was spiritual. Sometimes it was emotional, and sometimes it was all of the above.

Breaking can feel like the hardest thing you will ever go through, but I learned that it is also the most necessary thing you will ever go through. Amid the pain, I finally realized that the weight of the situation wasn't breaking me. It was readjusting me. It was rearranging my mind, body, and spirit in preparation for what was to come. When you are experiencing the pain of breaking, you tend not to see the meaning and learn from the thing that broke you. But that is where the true blessing lies.

As I think back over the breakings of my life, I realize that these painful experiences make me fit to help others. I can speak on the roads I have walked before, and I offer some guidance on where others are headed. I could be that word of warning someone else may need, but that wouldn't have been possible if I'd never experienced those breakings.

Think about how doctors fix broken bones. They readjust and put them back together. The breaking of the bone hurts, and the readjustment is uncomfortable, but on the other side, the bone is whole again. A breaking can make you feel like damaged goods, but in reality, that could not be farther from the truth. You are never broken beyond repair because there is no fall that you cannot recover from. My mom always says to me, "Once you hit ground zero, there is only one place to go, and that's up." Start working your way back up, and you will begin to understand that the toxicity that broke you before is no longer welcome in your life.

Start to see those breaking times as a restructuring that prepares you to go places you have never been before. Nobody wants to be broken, but when that breaking moment does come, allow it to take place, knowing that your roots are going to be replanted and grow even stronger.

THE DEEPER WE DIG

Sometimes, I ask God for a blessing and then feel dissatisfied when He answers my prayer. I ask for someone who loves me, but I don't want that person when He sends someone. I ask to make six figures. Then, He sends me a new job, and I'm mad at the amount of work it requires. I want a house, but the place He blesses me with needs many renovations. We have to work for the things we want, and the deeper we dig, the taller we can stand when those challenges arise.

A tall stance requires a deep foundation because the substance on the bottom is what ultimately holds you up during those tough times. When it feels like you're in a dark place, know that you haven't been buried; instead, you've been planted. With a plant, everything on top is breakable. You can easily pull it off, or it may even fall away on its own. But if you want to pull it up from the roots, you will have a much harder time because the roots are grounded so deeply under the surface. The stronger the roots, the stronger the plant stands.

I look at the abuse my mother experienced and how hard she worked to get what we needed. As I see her through my adult eyes, I realize the roots I come from. She has not waivered regardless of how the wind has blown. The things that I used to think were weak about her, I now know they were her strengths. She showed me that I could not just be blown with the wind, and I must be able to sustain something. I am my ancestors' wildest dreams because I am rooted in them. I am the root of the future generation, so I cannot be blown in the wind. When you are grounded and appreciative of your roots, you can stand tall in the midst of every storm.

When the pressure is on, and emotions are high, we each have a choice in how we respond.

—*Pastor Robert Madu*

Self-care is an ongoing process, but you must take the time to make it happen.
What have you done for yourself lately?

THE PRESSURE TO PERFORM – FAMILY

I am the youngest of four children in my family, but I've never felt like it. That's because I was never allowed the freedom to make the mistakes that my older siblings made. Instead, I was placed on an invisible pedestal topped by glass ceilings that everyone expected me to break. I grew up feeling pressure to perform from my whole family. My dad wanted his children to reach goals that he couldn't accomplish, and my mom adopted the same mindset. But you know how parents like to use that trial-and-error method. They teach the first child something, and when it doesn't work, they try a different technique with the second one. By the time they got to me, fear was the technique of choice. And it worked.

I grew up fearful about many things, but I was scared to death of failure. I felt like I was never good enough, no matter what I did. I was constantly striving for a mark that was not clearly articulated or defined for me. I knew that my father wanted me to get an education, so I earned five degrees. My mother wanted me to make a lot of money, so I worked to create a successful career. My siblings wanted me to be great because they saw something in me that I didn't see in myself. Even when they were growing up in the Detroit streets, they shielded me from the dangers of the hood. For many years, I carried the heavy obligation of making it for everyone. I had to change my perspective about the pressures my family placed on me.

First, I had to learn to take care of myself. I realized that I could not be good for anyone else without attending to my needs first. We often get so weighed down in giving ourselves to everything and everyone that there is no space left for us. But it is a trick of the enemy to stretch yourself so thin that you make no time for yourself. Your mental health and wellbeing are just as valuable as anyone else's. You can pour into yourself with the love and grace you deserve when you realize that.

The second thing I did was acknowledge my accomplishments and recognize the value I've brought to my family. Through my hard work and commitment, I have changed the entire tone of our family's legacy. I broke through those glass ceilings and earned the education that my father wanted for me. We have a doctor in our family, and for generations to come, everyone, who bears the last name Hemphill will know that they too can break the ceilings and achieve their goals. They will have a blueprint for changing the narrative, which subconsciously was precisely what I was trying to do.

The pressure to perform is real, but you cannot let your family's expectations overtake you. Change your perspective and recognize the value you already bring. Protecting my family is no longer an unbearable pressure to perform. Instead, it is my honor.

THE PRESSURE TO PERFORM – SELF

When looking at the big picture, we have pressure from family and society, and we set these expectations and timelines on ourselves. Some days, the pressure to perform that I place on myself is so heavy that I have to take a step back and breathe. All things you are forcing in your life will eventually come together, but not if you are in the wrong mindset… not if you are tripping over yourself and rushing instead of giving yourself some grace and rest. As you're rushing to perform, you may end up missing the jewels that God has sent your way.

I consider myself as a person who has been there and done that. I want to make sure I leave no stone unturned and everything on the table. In releasing the pressure to perform, I've had to break those cycles of unrealistic expectations that I have set up for myself. I had to start looking at myself more clearly through a different set of lenses that would allow me to be authentic to who I am. I had to learn how to stop trying to show up for every single person in my life, so I would have the energy to show up for myself.

Like so many others, I failed to recognize the strength and abilities that God had already gifted me. Moses thought he was walking around here with just a staff, not knowing the power that he held in the palm of his hand. How many of us are walking around here with the very thing to change the world and not using it because we are so focused on reaching these unattainable expectations that we set for ourselves? We are constantly trying to perform better instead of recognizing and leveraging the power that we already possess. Much of the pressure you feel from yourself to perform is about appearances rather than living in your true authenticity.

RECOVERING FROM TRAUMA

There have been moments in my life when I wanted to get even with people who have hurt me, offended me, or taken advantage of me. I wished hurt and harm upon them. I had to check my heart though. I had to realize that my need for revenge came from a selfish place, a place of hurt and anger. I also had to realize that there had been times in my life when I was the one hurting and offending people and thank the Lord that I did not get what I observed in those moments. God gave me the peace to let those vengeful feelings go through those realizations. No one gets away with anything in this life. Some people believe in karma, but I also realize that vengeance is the Lord's. I wanted God to deal with my abusers in a way that would break them down. But those thoughts were coming from a broken person. As I started to heal and become whole, I stopped wishing harm and started asking God to bless those who offended me. The same grace and favor that I want God to give to me, I asked for them.

The more I dealt with myself, the more I started to take small steps to deal with my trauma. I started recognizing how the traumas in my life had led to low self-esteem and anger. I asked God to take that hurt out of my life to forgive myself and the people who harmed me. There are still a lot of traumas there, but I take my recovery one day at a time. The more I go to therapy, read self-help books, and reflect on myself, the more I learn. I know my triggers. I know what spaces I can and cannot go into. I know which people I can be around and which ones I can't.

When dealing with trauma, you have to do the work. It's not an overnight thing that happens instantly. You have to work on it daily. People will tell you to hurry up and heal or hurry up and let it go. But it's not always that easy. It's something you have to work through. You have to survive the trauma and outlive it. Don't allow other people to put a timeline on how you recover from your trauma. Do the work and give yourself time to heal.

SAYING NO

Saying no has never been an easy task for me, mostly because I am a people pleaser. I've spent my entire life trying to please everyone around me instead of protecting my peace. I had to learn how to move differently. I learned how to say no and understand that no is not a bad word. So many times in my life, being told no turned out to be a blessing. What felt like rejection ultimately turned out to be for my protection, So, I eventually learned how to appreciate them.

At this season in my life, I'm learning to appreciate my no. I no longer question why I said no or waste time feeling guilty for my decision. Instead, I take my yes as a meaningful yes and my no as a significant no. I'm learning to find refuge in saying no.

I searched for a way to say yes, even when it didn't feel right in my spirit. But sometimes you need to look for the no. I find a piece of myself in every no, both those I receive and those I give. I had to teach myself that saying no was okay if it wasn't done with malice. Sometimes, you can't do what's being asked of you. There have been times when I've done cartwheels for people because I was trying to say yes. But saying no establishes needed and necessary boundaries. Some people will never consider your space or respect your needs because they're so focused on themselves. You have to respect yourself and say no to establish your limits and protect your peace.

REST

My mom used to say, "I was asleep, but I wasn't resting." You can have so much on your mind that your brain is still working even while asleep. So often, we hear people talk about how tired and exhausted they feel. When I hear that, I usually equate it to not getting eight hours of sleep the night before. But rest is not only tied to when you close your eyes. Rest is when there is an alignment between who you are authentically, spiritually, and naturally. It is when your whole being can quiet itself.

There is a quote that says, "I'll rest when I'm dead." I disagree with that sentiment. I believe that you can hustle, rest, and enjoy life all at the same time. So many of us allow other things to hinder our rest because we don't know how to let things go and ease our minds. To truly find rest, you must get to a place of categorizing what is important and what is not. What requires your attention and what does not require your attention. When you experience real rest, you find peace and balance within your life and who you are authentically.

Think about the serenity prayer. God, grant me the serenity to accept the things I cannot change, courage to change the things I can, and wisdom to know the difference. This is a place of balance. It is having a mindset to find peace and solace in every situation. We put so much on ourselves and controlling that when we do experience balance or peace, we do not even recognize it.

I have tried things like hot yoga or soul cycle when seeking rest. When I was so focused on the task at hand, I found that I could not let my mind wander to all of the other things outside of that task. Your road to rest lies solely within you. It's wherever you find comfort, where no external force hinders you from experiencing balance. It could be laying on the couch, washing the car, or even cooking a full course meal on a Thursday night. Whatever you need to do to ease your mind and relax, take a moment to rest and get to a place of wholeness.

SELF-CARE

Self-care hasn't always been a priority in my life. In fact, I would say that I didn't discover self-care. Self-care discovered me. That's because I didn't know how to do the simple things. I didn't see the value in keeping my hair cut or getting my nails done. When I think back on it, it feels kind of strange that I felt that way because my mom and dad were always serious about taking care of their appearances. It took a while for me to get it though. I didn't understand that the physical aspects of my life directly correlated to my mental wellbeing. Once I realized that, I understood the importance of getting a haircut or making an effort with my clothes. I know people say that your outside shouldn't dictate how you feel, but in reality it totally does.

The exterior can reflect what you're feeling on the interior and vice versa. Our outside is the cover of the book. The inside contains what we have been through. When we start to feel stress, it comes out as blemishes, lines, or even illness.

Your first priority should always be from the stance of self-care, and don't let people convince you that self-care is a selfish notion. I look at self-care from a standpoint of service to others, not just service to myself. If I am not taking care of myself, I'm no good to anyone else. What is there to give when you have nothing? The more I began to understand that the better care I took of myself.

Hopefully, you have someone you love and care about and want to be there for. Self-care is taking a moment to take care of yourself and make sure that from a mental, and physical, and emotional standpoint, you're okay to take care of someone else. Self-care helps you discover who you are so you can move differently in the world. If I tell my mother I am having a bad day, she will ask me if I have a haircut. It's just like making your bed. Caring for yourself can be the simplest thing, but it sets you up to go after the big things you want to accomplish.

Unfortunately, some of us use self-care to try and cover up what is really going on in our lives. I think this is a major issue within the Black community. My mother would always say, "What happens in my house stays in my house," and she did everything she could to make that happen. I remember watching my mom curl her hair, put on makeup, and keep it moving as if my dad hadn't just given her a black eye. I have seen my dad come home drunk and high, to the point where I could smell the crap coming out of his pores, but he would get up, get dressed up, and go to work like nothing was happening. It was always important to them to give off this persona that they had held it all together even though they were both hurting inside.

But that brings me to an even more important part of self-help, which is getting the help you need for mental health. Some of us are so quick to say, "I don't need therapy. I have God." Yes, you do have God, but you may still need some extra help to take care of your thoughts and emotions. Your pastor and your first lady are not your therapists. Your best friend is not your therapist. Getting the self-care we need requires us to step out of our comfort zone and do things we don't usually do. If that means going to a therapist, so be it. It will make you better for you and for everyone who loves you.

Changing the World

Changing the world is easy... believing you can change the world is something totally different...It is our duty to make the IMPACT needed to shift this world.

—*Dr. D.*

IMPACT = Individual Making Progressive Achievement and Continuous Transformation.

What transformations are you making in preparation to change the world?

DESIGNATED SURVIVOR

When we think about the trials and tribulations of life, we tend to see them as obstacles sent to keep us from reaching our goals. But we need to look at our difficulties in a whole new way. The negative things that we experience in life aren't there to stop us. They are there to create a battleground in our minds where we can stand despite the cards we are dealt – despite all of our shortcomings and despite how we view ourselves. See, you are still here. Those obstacles didn't stop you. In fact, they probably made you stronger. We have to shift our mindsets from a deficit standpoint to a place of honoring and celebrating our survival. The designated survivor mindset grows out of an understanding that it isn't always about what you've been through. It's about what you have survived.

We have a saying in the Black community that goes, "I don't look like what I have been through." And I don't. I have been through years of hell and high water, but I'm still here with more work to be done. Just like me, you are still here because you have a job to do and people out there who need what only you can offer. They need to feel inspired by your example and to learn the insight you have gained. They need to hear your stories – and not just the pretty ones – but the ones about the ugliness that you survived. We have to talk about the scratches and scars on our knees and the knots on our heads. We have to talk about the heartbreak, betrayal, and sleepless nights. We have to talk about all of the bad so we can appreciate that we are still here.

As a designated survivor, you may find yourself asking God, "Why are you preserving me? What is it that you are accomplishing through me?" And even if you don't receive those answers right now, trust in the fact that God always has a plan. We see designated survivors all throughout the bible. Jesus was a designated survivor. If Satan had the smallest glimpse of who Jesus was, he probably would have never crucified him. His dynasty was further established by his death. The devil thought that killing him would end his story, but 2000 years later, we are still worshipping him and his everlasting survival.

When we shift our thinking, we can recognize the value and opportunity that comes along with being a designated survivor. For me, it means that I am the one to change the narrative in my family. I will close the chapter on low self-esteem and feelings of inadequacy. I will open doors of opportunity for those who come behind me. The fact that I am still here means that there is still so much more for me to accomplish… and I know that there is much more for you to accomplish too.

CHANGED THINKING / CHANGED LIFE

My thinking patterns used to be really messed up. As a Virgo, I tend to overthink and overprocess everything. I was constantly in my head about degrees… and titles… and exes… and the pressure to perform. All of it weighed me down because I didn't know how to balance it all. I learned that I had to shift my thinking and refocus because my overthinking was guiding me to a place of deep frustration and discontentment. I was always focusing on the "what-ifs" and worrying about the future instead of living in the right now. I had to finally step back and realize that I can only deal with one issue at a time. Staying in your head too long will cost you something. It will cost you your relationships. It will cost you your sanity. It will cost you your peace.

If you don't control your mind, you will become a prisoner to your own thoughts. You have to empty that recycle bin in your head sometimes. Think about your email inbox. When there are too many messages, you reach your limit and you have to get rid of some of them. The same thing happens with your thoughts and mental space. You reach your limit. When that happens, you have to find a way to clear your head. For me, that's physical activity. I take my dog, Austin, for a walk or go for a run. I used to read books or listen to Ted Talks, but I found that those things put me right back into my maze of thoughts. Running helps me relieve myself of the pressure of constantly trying to process random judgments and scenarios. Instead, it allows me to focus on my run or on my dog. For you, it may be getting a massage or meditating. Whatever it takes, you need to change those harmful thinking patterns to change your life.

There is an internal war that sometimes takes place within our heads. When we allow that war to continue, we allow it to shake our peace and stability. Give yourself permission to live. I recently did something I'd never done before. I went skydiving. That's right. I, Danarius Hemphill, jumped out of a plane. In that moment of free falling to earth, all of the fear and anxiety left my head. There was no room to take on the cares of the earth or to think about all the negatives in life. In that moment, I realized that nothing was as bad as I made it seem in my head. The experience helped me prioritize and really understand what I appreciate the most in my life. Now, I am not telling you to go jump out of a plane, but I am telling you to take a moment and just breathe. Give your mind a break by changing your thinking process and you will change your life.

THE WORLD NEEDS GAME CHANGERS

The world needs more people with the wherewithal to stand up and be vocal… but not just be vocal. There also needs to be intentionality behind their words. We need more innovators who are willing to go against the grain to create and impact the entire world. We are in the midst of consistent change. From a technology standpoint, the world is constantly evolving. These innovations have only come about because of brave people who were not afraid to get it wrong and keep on going. We need more of those types of people… people with enough courage to give a new perspective.

True game changers call everyone to the table, and that's missing in our society right now. We are experiencing an environment where many of the people in power are intimidated by younger innovative leaders in the making. Current leaders are setting rules and policies that will impact generations without bringing other game changers to the table. They don't want to fall back and let new people come to the forefront. John the Baptist was already preparing a way when Jesus showed up on the scene. When he recognized who Jesus was, he realized that he needed to decrease as Jesus increased. He knew that he had done his job of paving the way, but he was not to be mistaken as the messiah. John the Baptist recognized that it was okay to take a back seat because the one who was called to be the ultimate game changer was on the scene.

When it comes down to changing the world, it starts with the individual. Before you can change the culture, you first have to change you, which is often the hardest part. Think about Moses. Moses grew up in Pharaoh's house as an Egyptian, yet he was born as a Hebrew. At some point he had to separate himself from being an Egyptian in order to be what he was destined to be, which was a Hebrew.

Game changers are not defined by their environment or limited by their experiences. It's not that they forget what was, but they understand that what was does not define what could be. They appreciate the right now but have foresight for things to come. A lot of leaders in high profile positions are not willing to hold themselves accountable and evolve with the times. They are so tied to what was, that they hinder what could be by refusing to shift their mindsets. This is not the kind of leadership we need. Authentic game changers challenge themselves and don't hesitate when called to the carpet. These are the types of strategic change agents that the world needs right now.

Impacting the world requires changing ourselves and lighting the match in others. When we set our intentions on helping society and changing the world, we can create an environment where game changers are constantly being birthed.

IT DOESN'T HAVE TO BE BIG. IT JUST HAS TO BE EFFECTIVE

When you strive to reach other people through your thoughts and actions, the steps you choose to take do not have to be big and grand. They only have to be effective. Reaching two or three people may not seem like much to you, but it's time to change your perspective. If you only reach one or two people and those people reach two more people, there is your effectiveness. You may not see it where you are, but that doesn't mean it's not happening. It only takes a single moment of impact to spark a chain reaction.

We often want the things we do to have to have a massive impact. We act out of a desire for notoriety and wanting to be seen. Yet, when you do what you are called to do and move from a place of love, notoriety and recognition take a backseat to your desires to help others. In everything I do, I never underestimate the power in reaching just one person.

Think about Bill Gates or Mark Zuckerberg. They both started off small. They could not have possibly seen how massive their efforts would become. Yet, they heard their callings and they acted on them. You must do what you are called to do out of the purity of your heart. When your intentions or motives aren't pure, it can negatively affect your impact. If you're doing it for fame or to see your name in lights, remember that light requires heat and heat requires pressure. Be mindful about the attention you think you want because you may not be as ready as you think you are for all that comes along with it.

When I started on this book writing journey, I had to ask myself if I was ready to reveal so much of my life. I had to make sure that my efforts were coming from a pure place instead of a place of attention seeking. I didn't want to write for the purpose of impressing people. I wanted to write for the purpose of expressing my thoughts and lessons. Boastfulness and pride can get in the way sometimes and have people going extra hard for fame. But fame is not where the prize ultimately lies. There are plenty of people working behind the scenes to impact others' lives. They go hard for their calling without regard for the spotlight. So, just remember that whatever you choose to do… it doesn't have to be big, it just has to be effective.

CHECKMATE

My journey is far from over. I am still trying to reach wholeness and clean up some of the rooms in my house. I still ask myself, "What is it that you want Danarius?" And I still don't know how to answer that question. In one breadth I feel like God has forgotten about me, but in the very next breadth I think God has me in the cut. Right now he is hiding me and moving me and preparing me. He did the same thing with Moses. He hid Moses right under Pharaoh's nose. The person who is going to disrupt your kingdom is right in your house. He did that with Saul too. The person who is going to bring forth the kingdom is right under your nose.

My appointed time just hasn't come around yet, but when it does, He will bring me out.

One of my friends explained it like this. There is a hierarchy in the kingdom of God. And it's imperative that I understand how the hierarchy is structured. There is a need for me to change my viewpoint and my perspective of myself and to adjust my lenses to the way that God sees me. My pastor would compare it to a harness on a child. I'll let you walk a little on your own, but I will pull you back if you try to go too far. Whom the Lord loves, HE chastens. God's chastisement of us is confirmation that we are His children. As God's children, there are some things He simply won't allow us to do...and I'm so glad about that!

That's where God has me right now. In that cut with a little bit of walking room. When He is ready to put me out there, all of the hurt and abuse that I've experienced in my life will be revealed as preparation. It's going to allow me to speak to that in others. Truth be told, I know I know what he called me unto, but I keep saying no I don't want that. I am being called to be a prophet, and though I keep saying "No, I ain't no prophet," I am recognizing that a prophet is a mouthpiece and servant of God. I have grown accustomed to being a servant and the more I tap into that role, the more I discover new gifts and abilities in helping others' visions become a reality.

My first lady said that the reason I moved away from Detroit was because no one would know who I am. They wouldn't know about the light that God has placed in me and expect anything from me. But she said that it doesn't matter which room I go into… I will expose who I am as soon as I open my mouth. It's basically me warring with me.

So here I am giving in to the Divine power. It is me saying the war is over. I played the game. I wore the veil. I threw the cloak over my head, but now the hiding and God's preserving me is over. The run is over and the race is won. I have the gold medallion and now it is time for God to expose me to the world. In this season, there is no more giving people an illusion of Danarius. This is Danarius. Check Mate. It's your move.

DESTINY IS NEVER WITHOUT DIFFICULTY

There is an inaccurate notion that we should be able to reach our purpose without difficulty. I've been guilty of it myself by thinking that things should not be as complicated as they are. I am doing God's will and trying to walk into my purpose, but it seems like I take one step forward and ten steps back. Even when it's within reach, I can't reach it. It's attainable, but I can't attain it. When we reach these crosswords, we tend to point all of the fingers at ourselves. We ask what we are doing wrong. Is this really my passion? Am I not doing something I am supposed to do? Sometimes we get frustrated with God and say I'm trying to achieve what you want me to achieve, but there are constantly barriers in the way. Why are you making it so hard?

But in the process of reaching your destiny, don't view difficulty as a hindrance. It may be part of the process to make sure you don't get somewhere too soon, before you are ready to be there. Sometimes we want to get to a destination quickly. We have an urgency to get there, but that urgency is ours and not God's. So what we see as difficulty is actually God managing the process. Sometimes, you have to be held or pulled back for a moment before you are launched into your next level.

For me, I am going through a process of having a child through surrogacy. Every day, I think about how badly I want my baby right now. But there is a reason why I'm going through this process. It takes planning and preparation to get where I'm trying to go. I have to prepare myself physically, emotionally, and mentally.

There is a cost that has to be paid for your destiny, but are you willing to pay it? Everyone wants the reward, but you must pay the price for it. You do yourself a disservice when you expect to walk into your destiny without paying the price.

So, when it comes down to reaching your purpose, know that difficulty is part of it. You can't have day without the night. You can't have the sun without the night. They are equally weighted because they are part of the process. You just can't reach your destiny without some difficulty.

Authenticity

Your time is limited, so don't waste it living someone else's life. Don't be trapped by dogma—which is living with the results of other people's thinking. Don't let the noise of others' opinions drown out your own inner voice. And most important, have the courage to follow your heart and your intuition. They somehow already know what you truly want to become. Everything else is secondary.

—*T.D. Jakes*

What goals are you setting today to
remain true to who you are?

Authenticity has been the key to my success! Mastering the art of being uniquely me has caused me to have lasting relationships & given me access to people I never imagined sitting with. Being authentic has granted me a seat at the table & each year I set a goal to remain true to who I am.

—*Dr. D*

REAL LUXURY IN INNER PEACE

We tend to have a fabricated view of luxury. We see it as the big house, the expensive cars, the fancy clothes, and everybody knowing our name. But luxury is not actually about the things you accumulate. It's about the peace that you create in your life. On any given day, I prefer to sit in my house than to go out somewhere. I can kick off my shoes and relax because there is a peace that I experience when I step through my front door. I can leave the external stuff outside and proceed into the peaceful environment I have created for myself.

So many people aspire to keep up with the Joneses. Keeping up with the Joneses will cost you something, and sometimes it costs you your inner peace. Everyone says that they are willing to pay the price for luxury, but that price looks like worry. Worrying about not having enough money to make ends meet and how much those "luxuries" are going to cost you. When I look around at people who constantly flaunt what they have, they always seem less peaceful to me. They appear to be in a constant battle between what they want and what they need.

I focus on what I need, and the more I do that, the more peace I actually feel in my life. When you aren't keeping up with the Joneses, you can take care of yourself instead of spending your time trying to please or impress anyone else. It's a matter of priorities and making sure your priorities are right. It's not having two luxury cars and living in low-income housing. It's not walking around in fancy shoes when you can't pay the water bill. That is not a life that I desire or a legacy that I want to pass down to my future generations. When you recognize that real luxury lies in inner peace, you will live a more peaceful and luxurious life.

MAN EVOLVE

We live in a world where everyone wants things delivered quickly and easily – from food to wealth, and even salvation. But we have to recognize that what we want does not always come the way we expect. Evolution takes time, and it's not always comfortable. Just look at our phases of life. As we evolve from children into adulthood, our clothes and shoes become too small. Things that used to fit, don't fit anymore. The body of a pregnant woman goes through an evolution as bones begin to form in the womb and another heart begins to beat in the belly. Things that once seemed impossible become possible, but that change comes with some pain and discomfort.

Evolution doesn't happen according to your schedule or comfort. In fact, it usually happens when God abruptly interrupts your regularly scheduled program. And when it happens, it may require you to leave your home and everything you find familiar – to hop in the car with your puppy on a random day of the week and drive away as your mom stands in the driveway crying.

Leaving Detroit for Austin was one of the hardest moves of my life. I was hurt because I had to leave my family, my recently purchased home, and everything that I found comfortable. But I had asked God for promotion. I just had no idea that would come wrapped in a move to Texas. I tried my hardest to resist, and even looked for ways to stay, but God spoke to me.

He told me that it was time to evolve, embrace my assignment, and answer the call. I had to stop resisting and yield to the evolution taking place in my life. Sometimes, the enemy wants you to think you've lost everything when, in actuality, you have lost nothing and gained everything.

When God says it is time to move, it is time to move. When God says it is time to evolve, it is time to evolve. Answer His call and embrace your assignment wrapped in His blessed assurance.

WHOLENESS/ GO FOR BROKE

Wholeness is the destination of a lifelong journey. A whole individual is secure in his or her abilities and comfortable with their internal and external appearances. There is no shadow of doubt where they question who they are. They know who they are and they truly understand that. How dare we think that we come from a whole God but are not whole people. When I bring a child into the world, it is a whole being. Not a half being, and it's the same with God. There is no lacking in you because He has given you all that He is.

Wholeness is no longer questioning who you are and what you are called to do. You no longer question whether or not you're ready to walk into your destiny. You finally recognize that you are on a journey of evolving into who you are spiritually called to be. Wholeness is a level of confidence where there is no insecurity or wrestling with self-discovery.

Once you let go of all those negative thoughts and feelings, you can truly go for broke. There is no more sitting back and waiting for something to happen. You become willing to leave what feels comfortable to risk it all and discover who you truly are. You may not feel secure in the process, but once it's done, you will find security in your wholeness.

I always felt that my father looked at me with an elevated expectation of greatness. He expected me to achieve all of the goals that he had not been able to reach. When he saw me, he saw wholeness. But when he saw himself, he saw incompletion. I don't want to see incompletion in me. He didn't want me to see incompletion in me. I want wholeness in me so I can pass that on to my child. I want him to see wholeness in me and I will see wholeness in him. As the Bible says, when you see the father, you see the son and when you see the son, you see the father. Even though my pastor isn't my natural father, people always tell me that they see him in me when I speak. They tell me that my thinking patterns mirror his, even though my attitude and demeanor come from my natural father. This has helped to give me my wholeness. I am a merger of my natural father with my spiritual father.

When I say go for broke, do all of the things we have discussed in this book. Take all of it and decide that, come hell or high water, you are going to move forward in your wholeness. People may like the idea of who they thought you were, but it's time for them to experience who you really are and who you are not. You've been waiting on someone else to make a move, but it is time for you (and me) to make the ultimate move. There has to be a level of consistency and a commitment not to return to those habits and connections that held you back. That umbilical cord must be cut in order for you to grow and become who you are destined to be. Don't underestimate the urgency of this matter because it is easy to go backwards. That comfort can be addictive, but you can't do that anymore. You must cut away who you used to be and come into who you are supposed to be.

ENOUGH IS ENOUGH

When you get comfortable with people disrespecting you, you send a very dangerous message. Whether you realize it or not, you are subconsciously declaring that you are not worthy of their respect, and even worse, that they can stay in your life even though they mistreat you and refuse to recognize your worth. When you allow yourself to be treated badly, you're basically cheating on you. You're ignoring your own worth and allowing others to do the same. But there must come a time when you say enough is enough. Look at the people who constantly disrespect you. Think about your history with those people and their actions over time. Chances are that there was never a level of respect to begin with. They do what they do because you have allowed it to go on without consequences.

This is a lesson that I still struggle with as I enter into new relationships. I've had to become more mindful of people's agendas and realize that those agendas are often not as pure as I thought they were. I had to learn how to restrict some people's access to me. I know that may sound harsh, but it's not a bad thing. It's a necessary thing for my peace of mind and growth. In addition to looking at their agenda, I had to start examining my own. What about me allowed this disrespectful person to attach themselves to me? What about me allowed that person to continuously mistreat me? What kept driving me to people and things that ultimately ended up hurting me? I had to recognize the role I played in these unhealthy relationships, identify the underlying issue, and deal with it.

When we cheat ourselves, it is always tied to something we have never dealt with in the past. We have to do the work of peeling back the layers and examining why we allow ourselves to be treated that way. We could be so much farther along in our destiny if we stop cheating ourselves. If we declare that we have had enough, we can start to own our worth and validate ourselves. The work takes time. It is not a microwave situation that provides a quick fix, but the more effort we put into the work, the more gratification we give to ourselves.

Too often, we give authority to people who don't deserve it. People who make us feel drained, broken, and inadequate. It is time to take back that authority and walk away from those people. You have to take a stand on what you will and will not tolerate. The more you get accustomed to living that way, the more you will recognize and value your self-worth. When you know your worth, you surround yourself with people who truly route for you and want to see you succeed. Don't wait until the disrespect and mistreatment beats you down or gets you to the point of acting out of character. Declare that enough is enough, recognize your power, and demand your worth.

THE LIE AND THE TRUTH

Throughout my life, I have been constantly lying to myself and telling myself that I was not ready to be who I have been called to be. You may be continuously telling yourself the same lie. You have convinced yourself that you are incapable or ill-prepared to move into your destiny, but that is all a lie. The truth is, you are ready. You've already made it this far, and there is no more preparation needed. Not one more book, Ted Talk, or speaker is going to make you more ready to move forward. The hour has come and it is time to move.

The enemy comes to do a few things… to kill, steal, and destroy. As the father of lies, he comes to hinder the process. He is the master trickster and the master of illusions. When we buy into those lies, we hinder our own progress and stop ourselves from reaching our true potential. We believe that we are not ready for something that is already predestined for us. At the moment you started taking form as a seed, God deposited everything that He meant for you to accomplish. There was no incapability placed into you. He gave you all you need to reach your destinies.

We have to stop lying to ourselves and disconnect from the lies in order to step into our promise. We are all connected in this world, and that includes our destinies. When we fight against our purpose in life, we could be stagnating, hindering, or postponing someone else's destiny. Right now, someone could be waiting on you to truly become you before they can truly become them. So, you must stop hesitating and going around the same mountain, like the Israelites did.

Your potential and who you are destined to be can happen right here and right now. You don't have to keep waiting. Just stop buying into the lies that other people keep telling you, the lies you keep telling yourself and the lies the enemy keeps telling you. The truth is that you are ready. The truth is that you are smart enough. The truth is that you are capable of starting your own business. The truth is that you are worthy of getting married and starting a family.

Everything you have a desire to accomplish, you can accomplish. If you couldn't, you would not have a desire to do it. Disconnect from the lie and connect to the truth.

PERFECT VS. AUTHENTIC

Perfect is nothing but an illusion. It is restricting. It limits you. It will stagnate you. It will kill you. Because you are striving to attain something that you were not designated, suited, or even equipped to accomplish. We are striving for a perfection that we are never going to be able to reach. There is only one perfect being, so who in the world told you that you have to be perfect? You can search all through the bible and you will not see one example of God calling His people to be perfect. But He did call them to be authentic.

Our blessings, our deliverance, our restoration, our elevation and our promotion come from our authenticity. They come from being true to who we are. I have written dissertations about being authentic, and it was so critical to my life because I didn't quite understand how to tap into my authenticity. I had to figure out how to remove all of the filters and stop trying to be perfect to realize that, if I am going to be who I am striving to be, it will only happen through me being honest with myself.

People always talk about keeping it real. But keeping it real will get you in trouble. Keeping it authentic will bless you and bless someone else's life. Authenticity comes from a place of humility because you aren't trying to be boastful or walk around with your chest poked out. Instead, you recognize that the place where you have arrived did not come easily. It came with bumps, bruises, and scars. And all of these experiences made you who you are today.

Perfection is the death of authenticity. It hinders you from becoming who you are truly designated to be. The fight we are engaging in – which we have been preparing for all of our lives – is to come to a place where we acknowledge that we don't have to have it all together. We admit that we are not perfect and we do not have to give the appearance that we are. Even when we talk about our success, we openly admit all of the battles that we won to get there.

When you are constantly trying to reach perfection, you have a deficit. You are in a relationship with an illusion of who you think you should be instead of who you truly are. You are turning yourself into a representative instead of appreciating your authentic self. We often send this representative out into the world because we are scared to show up as our real selves. Then we get into relationships with people who also put up a representative and miss out on having real relationships with truly authentic people. When you show up as your true self, you find out which people around you are also authentic. Escort your representative out the back door and welcome your authentic self through the front door.

This is the battle that you have been training for all of your life. The battle of recognizing how to dismiss the old version of who you used to be. Put your gloves on and get ready to fight because it's not easy getting rid of who you think you are to embrace who you are authentically. It won't happen overnight.

You may have been through a few rounds, but there is more to go before you reach that TKO where you knock that false version of you out of the ring.

This is a fight for your life. The bell is about to ring, the stage is set, and the stadium is full of old versions of yourself. Get ready to rumble!

ASK YOURSELF IF YOU HAVE: COMPLETE CONTROL, SOME CONTROL AND OR NO CONTROL

I have always had an issue with wanting to be in control. I expected to have control and I was usually the first to step up and exert control over a situation. But I had to learn a couple of important lessons about myself and why I always felt the need to be in control.

First, I realized that the only real control is having no control. I had to understand that there really isn't any control at all. Everything that you think you're controlling can change in an instant because all control belongs to God. When I accepted that fact, I stopped trying to control everything around me. I placed my trust in God and every aspect of my life became more glorious. I stepped out on faith knowing that God will always provide in His time. It was in those moments, when I relinquished my need for control, that I had my biggest successes.

The second thing I learned about my need to control was that I actually crave and desire the opportunity to give up my control. People perceive me as an individual who needs to have control, but I am constantly looking for reasons to give it up. I would be happy to slide this plate over to someone else because it's too full and all of my food is touching. People like me are often criticized as having a controlling mentality or spirit. But it's not that we have a controlling spirit, we are just waiting for others to come into the arena and pull their weight. If others would glow up, we would be more than willing to relinquish the responsibility of carrying everything on our own.

If you're like me and you find yourself trying to control the situations around you, take a moment to reflect on who you are and what you are intentionally trying to achieve. It's important to ask yourself that question because we all get so weighed down with the cares of life. Trying to be in control adds even more on your plate, possibly more than you have room to handle. When you try to handle too much, things start falling through the gaps. You may stop paying attention to the people and things you care about the most because you are too busy trying to control everything. You may find yourself being stretched beyond your capacity in a negative way.

So, ask yourself how much control you really have over any situation and realize that, in reality, it's closer to some or none. God is the only one with complete control over all variables. Let go of your controlling ways and trust Him.

YOU ARE A MASTERPIECE

So many times throughout my life, I have needed to remind myself how special and uniquely qualified I am – even for the things I believed I was unqualified for. It had nothing to do with my success or titles. It was ultimately just recognizing who I am from my foundation. God is the master artist and He created you, flaws and all, as a masterpiece. Much like artists stand back to admire their work, God steps back to look at us as His masterpieces, masterpieces that will forever change the world.

We focus on our so-called flaws – the lazy eye, the speech impediment, whatever we don't like about ourselves. Instead of seeing these differences as our uniqueness, we use them as an excuse. We tell ourselves that we cannot reach that goal or attain that level of success because of our flaws. But the truth is that God doesn't make mistakes and nothing about us was created in error. Those details that you see as errors may actually turn out to be your superpower. They could be the things that help you bless others and fulfill God's vision for you.

Have you ever felt like a second draft pick? I've felt like that many times. When faced with rejection, flaws, and failures, you can start to adopt a mindset of always being number two. Culture was constantly telling me that I had to be an alpha male. If I wasn't an alpha male, I was considered a beta male. Now, society means that as an insult to my manhood, but the funny thing about it is that I find solace in being the beta male.

Think about it. Most of the time, the alpha male gets it wrong. Adam got it wrong and because he got it wrong, Jesus came on the scene to bring order and new revelation. He had to correct the mess-ups that Adam – the alpha male – created.

Even in those times when you are made to feel like a second draft pick, you are always God's first draft pick. Being a masterpiece means reintroducing ourselves, not only to the world, but also to ourselves. That can be the most challenging part, but it is also the most necessary part. Recognizing your value does not require validation from anyone else. It solely depends on your view of yourself. We look for love and appreciation to validate who we are, but God has already given His stamp of approval to the fact that we are masterpieces, so never confuse others' validation with your self-worth. God has a designated plan in mind for each and everything He creates and that includes every single part of you.

I wonder how much our lives and the entire world would change if we could only see ourselves the way that God sees us. I challenge you to recognize, embrace, and fall in love with the masterpiece that God created within you.

CONCLUSION

Remember when you want different for yourself, you have to move different because those old keys will not unlock your new doors. We want authenticity, but to get it you have to release those old keys. Sometimes we work under the failed beliefs that we can continue doing what we have always done but get a different result.

This is not your normal book or devotional. It is going to take application, sacrifice, and most importantly, giving yourself to yourself. This book has not only come to challenge you. It comes to provoke you and give you what you're missing in your journey. It is inspiring you to live more. I want and need you to find your voice and live.

Life is about continuously evolving and recreating yourself. Explore, discover, and learn new things to add value and versatility to life. You shouldn't be who you were before reading this book. I hope that you have created new habits and consistently upgraded yourself towards your true authenticity.

This conclusion is not the conclusion. It is only the beginning of your journey. This is not a book that you place on the shelf and leave. You throw it in your makeup bag, your toolbox, or your designer bag and revisit as you apply it to the areas of your life where you need it to fit.

"If you enjoyed reading this, please leave a review on Amazon. I read every review and they help new readers discover my books."